BREXIT

IN A NUTSHELL

FOR ALL

Believer

and

I0490439

Not Believers...

By

Mary Lily P

Eliot Richards

NONSENSE?

Economically
speaking...
It does/ or it does not
make any sense!?

INTRODUCTION

Today the fate of one of the Greatest countries as it could happen to other one is on the stake.

As happens before in the history of every country, times are coming with challenges that expect sacrifices but real understanding and cold blood.

The inevitable decision of what to do not only in the coming elections is in the hands of its citizens and how they will vote to leave or to remain.

By the way, the history is repeating itself in this occasion are the Tory that is astonishingly leasing this country wealthy and powerful into Eden or the Hell.

No one should forget the bad e xperiences from the past. They are now the right time to show that the lessons from the past have learnt.

So, lets now revise what Brexit is, in a nutshell, wherefrom is it emerged? And if it is good or bad for this Great Nation.

The extraordinary
United Kingdom

UNITED KINGDOM AFTER BREXIT?

BREXIT...
WHAT FOR?

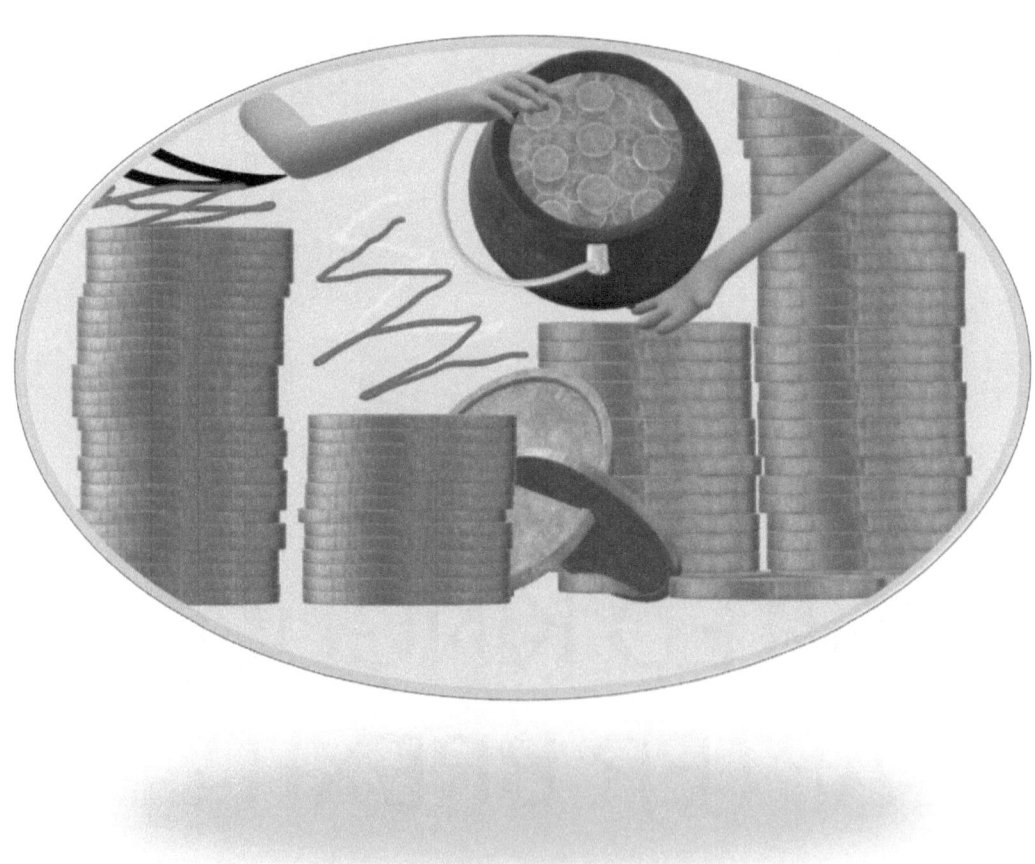

It is an obvious question, however, not many citizens are able to answer this question clearly and honestly, even now after three years of debate.

If we are still having in mind the previous pages, the idea of leaving has started right after the UK joined the EC, that is the EU today.

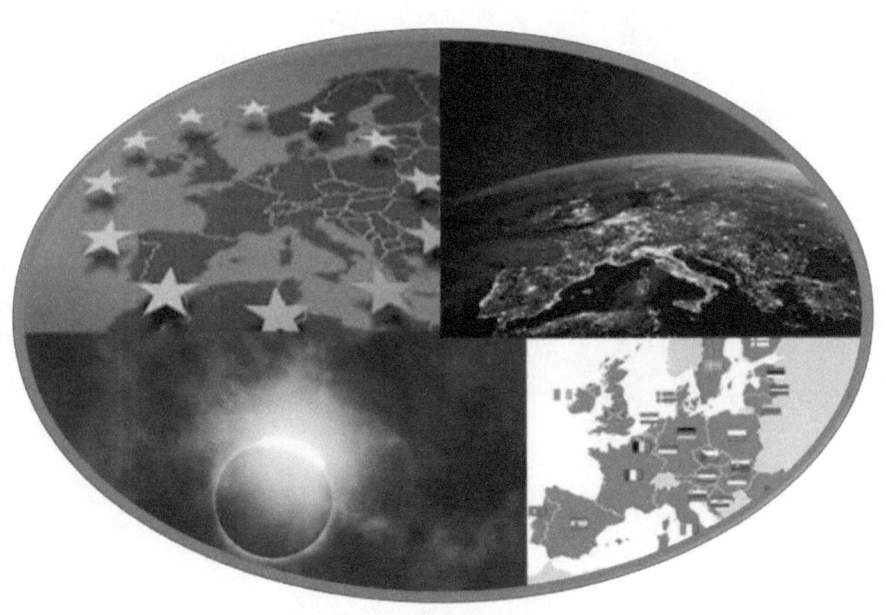

Guided by old dates and old dudes back then, members of one party were convinced that the deal of being part of the EC could be renegotiated as it was unfavourable to the UK, but the commitment was not enough, and they failed.

Such times were dubious times and full of crazy changing ideas.

WHAT IS THE BREXIT ANY WAY?

It might be something like British Exit if the word is decomposed in two.

Of course, is not just that, Brexit could be a lucky play or a disastrous one, it will depend on who lead the Brexit outcome and how wise such leaders will be.

The common definition is "Brexit is a movement that promotes that the United Kingdom (UK) leave the European Union (EU)", whereas the legal definition is: "is the scheduled withdrawal of the United Kingdom (UK) from the European Union (EU) after 2016, in which 51.9% voted to leave".

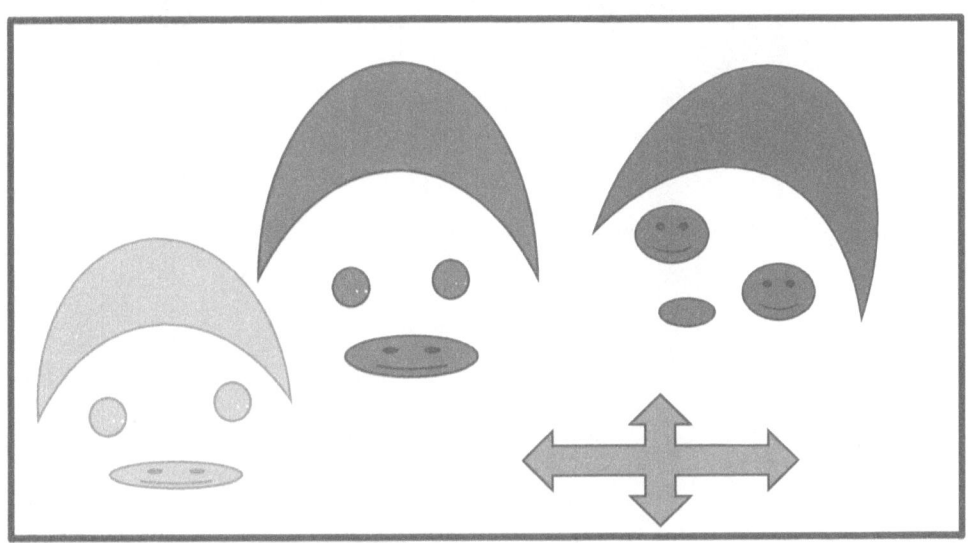

But stop here, to be frank, what happens, the will to leave is not new at all, this idea and struggle started a long time ago, **around the 70s then again in the 90s by others,** guided by different motives and political grounds.

Let's remember the UK government that in 1969 successfully applied for EC membership, and signed the Treaty of Accession in 1972 (Into Europe, 2017).

Here the struggle started, mainly, in 1975 the UK held its first-ever national referendum, to remain in the EC. Back then, 67.2 % voted to stay in (Miller, 2015). Recently in 1983 again the labour tried to leave without a referendum but desisted.

But it seemed that the idea did not die and in the 90s after EC evolved into the EU by becoming a political union from an economic union (EU treaties,2016), some countries disliked the idea.

In 1997, the Referendum Party to contest fight again but it died with his founder.

Finally, a party that since 1993 was gaining attention amongst voters achieved strong support to leave the EU in 2014.

LATER on, other issues like EC currencies and countries

own business needs and strategies created a new burden

to some EC countries, which were settled down over the

years, mostly with the creation of the Euro.

Nevertheless, the wounds and scars never cured or went

far away, and political ambitions made them a perfect

instrument for **discord** and **discussion** between EU

countries.

Closer to our time, and after Eurosceptics leaders gained

popularity, no without the help of some influential people

behind local media, the idea of a new "leave" has kept

conquering more supporters amongst clueless citizens,

and people with their owns agendas. Their strategy has

been to convince everyone that the profound British societal problems can be eliminated, by leaving the EU.

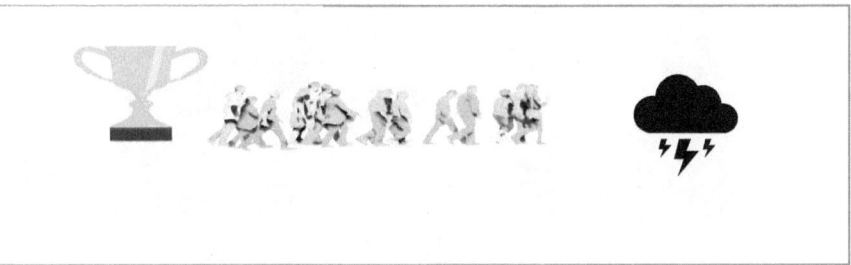

Thus, people obsessed with popularity finally scored a goal into British citizens' trust, transforming this beautiful and peaceful UK into a battlefield. A theatre of war because some citizens even threaten others without mercy, putting their real intentions to win the golden trophy over reason and country well-being.

This battleground has already made dysfunctional several politicians figures and is still causing chaos inside those different parties for ever without return.

However, the question "Brexit what for?", is still without a proper answer, appropriated to all living human beings under UK legislation, on this multicultural Island perpetuated in time, and space.

A GOD FOR ALL?

IS IT BAD?

IS MULTICULTURALISM GOOD FOR ALL?

WHO MAKES IT UP?

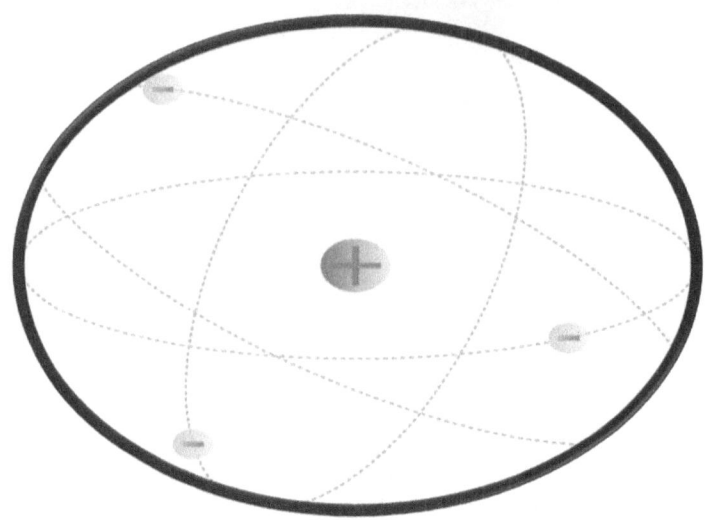

As we have already mentioned this idea-OF BREXIT- was born a long time ago just after the idea of joining the EC was achieved.

Since them, this idea was in the air, floating directly or indirectly in politicians mind and hearts.

For some it was just a solution to something, for others it was merely an excuse to get rid of things they did not want, and for some of them, it was the perfect way to win votes without a plan b.

As it was underlined earlier, the Brexit idea was born naturally in a political arena, and if it was ethical or biased….it will depend on who the judge is, and its criteria.

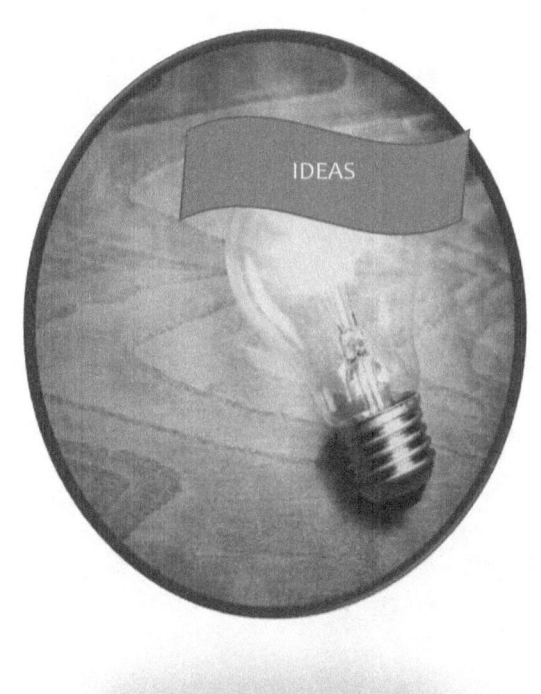

Politicians made up such ideas, in order to catch people votes. These views could be good or bad, depending on who accept them or dislike them.

The World needs ideas to keep developing. The issue is to create problems and disgust them as ideas to solve challenges that only exists in politicians' minds. This is the why it is important to understand such plans or proposals, the origins and most importantly, their consequences.

People voting should not take such ideas quickly, but with strict and responsible attitude because when such concepts are applied to our lives will be later and impossible to amend the irreversible and permanent damages.

HOW ABOUT CHILDREN... WHO REALLY CARE ABOUT THEIR FUTURE???

Think before voting!

Future generations could be grateful or could never forgive us, so let us this question again and again and try to answer it sincerely to our better knowledge no other knowledge.

The Ancient European continent and its states changed, new states disappeared, whereas others emerged as consequences of human tensions, and conflicts.

For centuries these states and populations evolved and prospered under the influences of world best minds, but also suffers from conflicts, wars, and diseases caused by the lack of sanity, order, and illiteracy, which were caused by authoritarian, ruthless rulers and dictators.

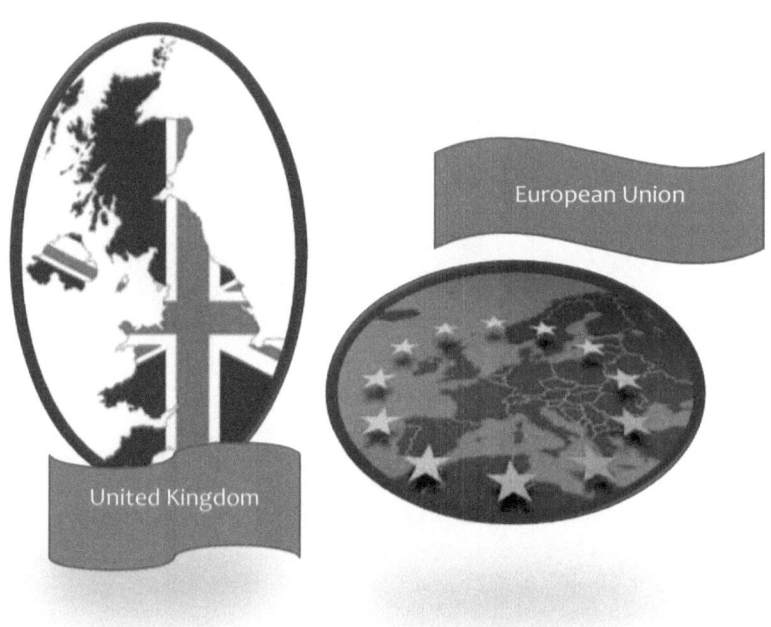

For instance, the Roman Empire grew expand and reached out its splendour only to degenerate and decline after being invaded by the Barbarian.

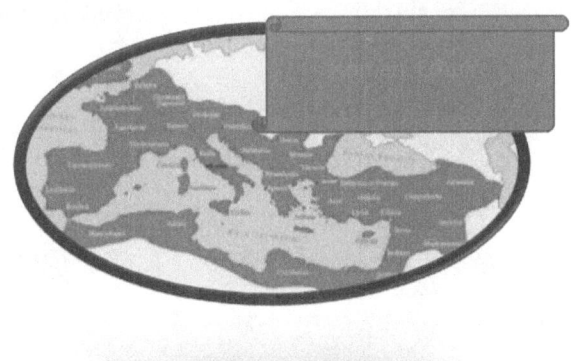

Nationalisms and religious philosophies also contributed to the escalation of conflicts that changed the World forever.

? Why   Why ?   Why?

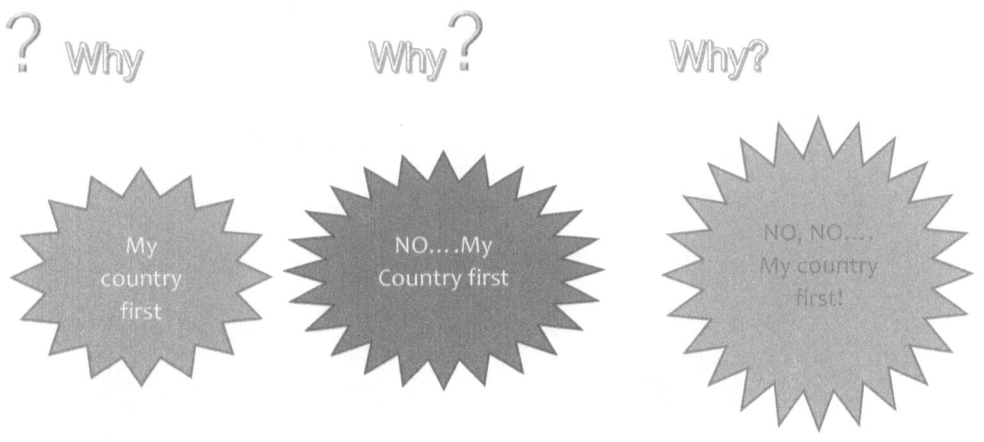

My country first

NO….My Country first

NO, NO,… My country first!

After two World Wars that left devastated our World is obvious **THAT WE WILL NO SURVIVE a** Third World War, because of nuclear power in the hands of insensible politicians all around the World

Our peaceful future is in our hands, therefore,

DO NOT WASTE IT.

What we need is a new human way to avoid future similar human disasters and destruction **NOT CREATE MORE EXCUSES FOR WARS.**

Here in Europe, such integration idea was

realised when the EC was created. Before was the

founding of the Council of Europe in 1949, then after that

the European Coal and Steel Community, followed by the

creation of the European Economic Community (EEC) in 1957 and the establishment of a customs union.

IT IS NOT PERFECT BUT WAS A GOOD START

European Economic Community (EEC)

The final step was the EU creation in 1993 with the enforcement of the Maastricht Treaty. The UK officially joined the ECC later called EU in 1972.

THE EUROPEAN UNION

LET'S THINK OF
A BETTER PLACE
BUT WITH OUR
HEART
NOT WITH OUR
HATRED.

UNITED KINGDOM FAILED BROTHERS

The British empire ceased to exist, and only historical and economic ties remained. The closest despite all odds remains the strongest.

We can live forever in the past, but this is insane and very bad for our Health and Prosperity.

The future is to stay together and face the challenges that already face the Earth.

Now we need to be together to save the planet, to tackle pollution, to protect our natural resources, to keep out unscrupulous politicians of our clean seas and lands.

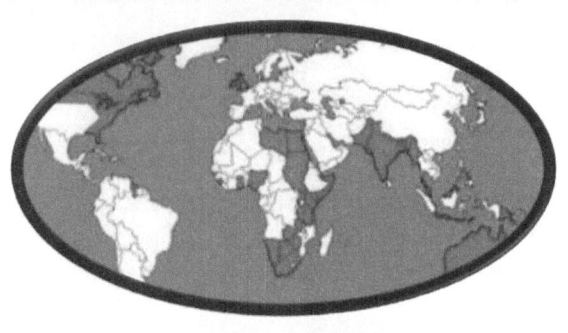

The new World for the UK becomes, a Commonwealth

back garden and the EU membership. The other

economics alternatives are regulated and to some extent,

limited by the EU treats.

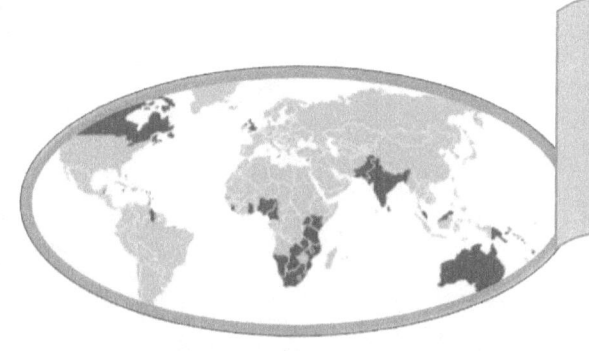

The former British colonies despite being in traditional trade became a more freely traders than before, and the intention of treating them as before like "colonies" will never be accepted by them again.

SO, A NEW APPROACH BASED IN MUTUAL RESPECT IS NEEDED.

The World has been changing, and The British Empire is gone forever

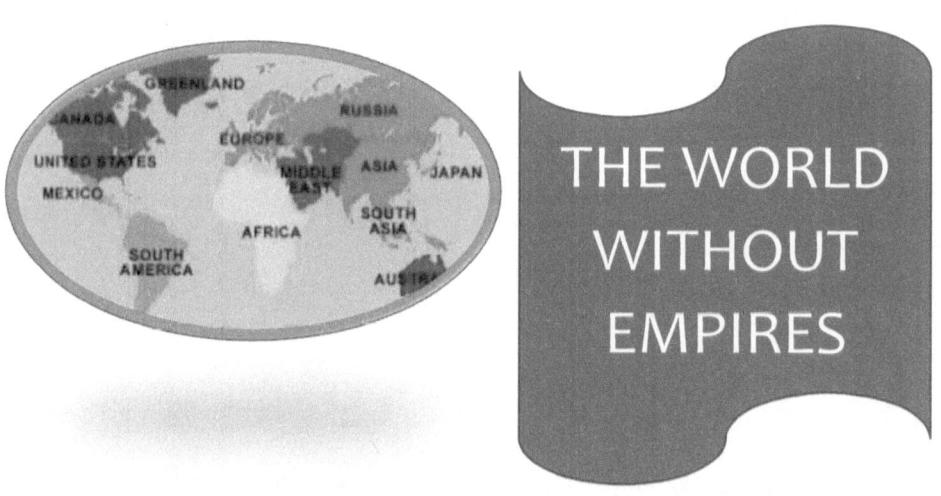

THE WORLD WITHOUT EMPIRES

Therefore, new globalised, real approach to World trade is needed, instead of the traditional one led by old-fashioned politicians and businessmen.

The relationship between the UK and other States like the USA, needs to be cautious,…let's just remember the history." In the mind of the average Englishman the picture of America is over-simplified … the American whom the Englishman was likely to meet before the outbreak of war was generally a visitor, a comparatively rich visitor at that … because of a slight xenophobia tinged with envy, the belief has arisen in the minds of many of those who have had only casual contacts with the Americans that they were rather assertive and arrogant." (Arnold, 2014)

BUT is BREXIT REALLY NEEDED RIGHT NOW

The European Union is not in good shape

no direction after making excessive expansion, showing signals of weakness, bureaucratization, excessive financial regulations, intrusion in EU state affairs and so on,

but it does not mean all states should leave, in the opposite more than ever EU states need to work together against all the odds and economics challenges.

For instance, individual states interests need to be re-evaluated in all dimensions.

In addition, new strategies new to be designed and implemented rather than keep fighting between the states themselves, otherwise EU will stop to serve as an organization that advocates integration… instead of

old problems such as

nationalism, radicalization…

will come back.

IS THIS OUR FUTURE?

... MORE WARS

The World needs *peace*

and

progress not wars, conflicts

and political egoism.

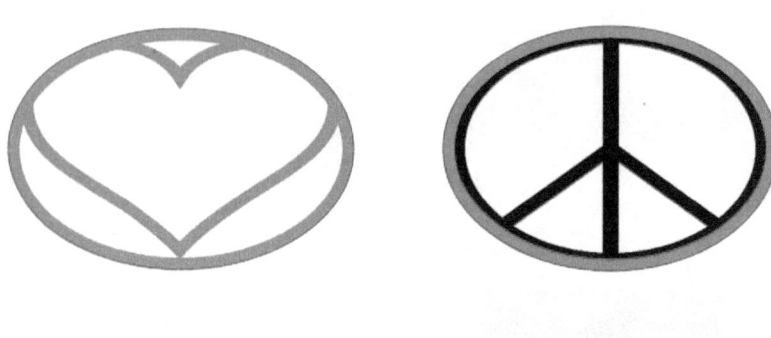

<u>AND</u>

Let's see the lack of unity

what is causing in the World

right now:

wars in the middle east, the

devastation and almost

demised of Syria,

the economic crisis of

Greece

Terrorist organizations trying

to destabilise Our World

A good example of politicians catastrophise is: **A civil war in Ukraine** between brothers, after more than 70 years of peaceful brotherhood, made up by **irresponsible leaders**.

WHOM BENEFITS FROM BREXIT?

Probably is a question that nobody wants to answer, but it is a vital- significant question that will define why Brexit becomes an obsession for ones and a thread for others.

Who can really benefit from Brexit?

directly-first of all:

1. POLITICIANS

BECAUSE THEY ALWAYS FIND THE WAY TO GET VOTERS INVOLVED
TO GAIN THEIR VOTES...

ADVICE:

THINK CAREFULLY WHOM you SUPPORT

BE SURE OF THEIR REAL INTENTIONS.

UNETHICAL BUSINESSMEN

GREEDY AND THIRSTY OF BEING UNMONITORED

BUSINESSPEOPLE THAN DO NOT CARE

ABOUT WORKING-HONEST PEOPLE, BUT THEIR INTERESTS AND PROFITS

A FEW VERY RICH PEOPLE

WHY?... BECAUSE IS NOT ENOUGH EVIDENCE THAT BREXIT WILL BRING ANY GOOD TO THIS AMAZING COUNTRY,

WHEREAS THERE IS EVIDENCE AND ECONOMIC DATA THAT SHOW THAT BREXIT WILL ECONOMICALLY AND SOCIALLY DISTRASOUS FOR THE UK

SOME PEOPLE MOTIVATED BY HATRED AND OLD-FASHIONED MENTALITY

Be careful of all those people judging people because of their nationalities.

People are not wrong just because of their nationalities- a foreigner here is not a foreigner in his/her country.

We, British citizens, we are not foreigners in the UK, but we are foreigners in Sweden, Spain, Italy …

WE ALL ARE FOREIGNS SOMEWHERE

ECONOMICALLY IS BREXIT A GOOD IDEA

If you are a naïve human being, YOU might find out reasons for considering

Brexit a solution to many problems of this beautiful country.

BUT THINK AGAIN
WHAT EXACTLY
WILL BREXIT BRING…

We have already Known:

More unemployment
The closing down factories

Companies out business caused by the natural social and economic development of our globalised World.

INSENSIBLE SOLUTIONS TO <u>HISTORIC PROBLEMS</u>

INMIGRATION IS NATURAL

...

NATURAL MIGRATION

from

THE FREE TRADE

WILL NEVER BRING

BETTER PARTNERS

OR MORE EXPORTS

FOR THE UK

BUT MORE

UNCERTAINTY

AND

A LOTS OF MORE

QUESTIONS

AND

NEEDS

THAT ARE

ALREADY SOLVED

WITHIN EU

AS TRADE

PARTNERS.

WE DO NOT

WANT

MORE WARS!!!

ON TOP OF IT,

UNSUSPECTED
THREATS

COULD PUT

THE UK
SECURITY at RISK
AT ALL LEVELS.

THE **ACHIEVED**

ADVANCE

IN ALL AREAS

GAINED

IN THE LAST 30

YEARS

IN THE EU

WILL BE LOST

FOREVER

FOR NOTHING

INSTEAD OF

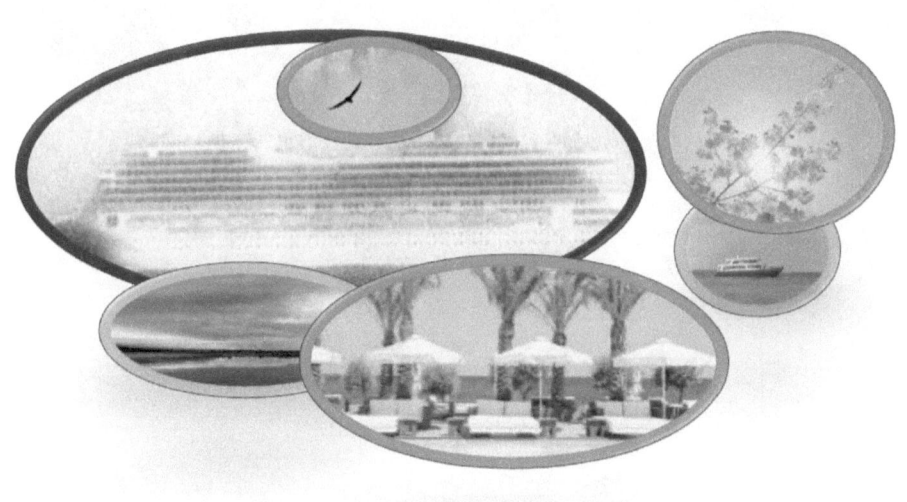

CAN BREXIT HELP WORKING-HONEST PEOPLE?

Imagine you are
in a place where
everyone can work
through
several countries
without limits
compare to a place
where such places
are so limited you

barely can find a
decent job.

LET'S SEE HOW ALREADY
FOREIGN COMPANIES
ARE CLOSING DOWN

CAUSING MANY JOBS
BEEN GONE

SMALL Businesses WILL
CLOSE DOWN or SURVIVE
ON THEIR OWN

THE TOURISM INDUSTRY WILL SUFFER HEAVILY THE PRICES OF FOOD THAT WAS IMPORTED FROM THE EU COUNTRIES WILL BE MORE EXPENSIVE DUE PRIMARILY TO NEW TAXES AND

CUSTOMS
REGULATIONS AND
EVEN MORE,
COMPANIES WILL
CHARGE MORE FOR
TRANSPORTATION
OF ALL PRODUCTS
THEN NEVER
BEFORE

THE WAGES WILL NEVER GO UP IN THE OPPOSITE THE WILL KEEP FALLING DOWN.

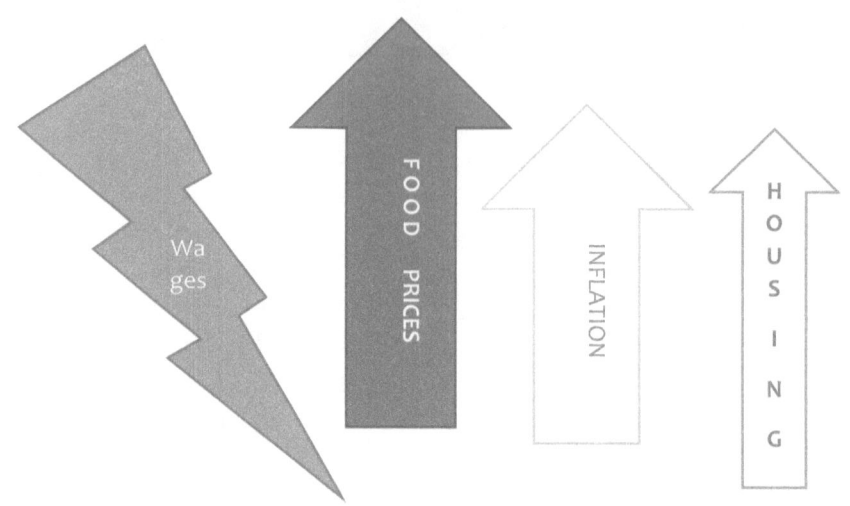

SO,

CHOOSE

WISELY

AND

GOOD

LUCK

Bibliography

Arnold, G (2014) *America and Britain was there ever a special relationship?* Washington: Blackwell.

Miller, V (2015). "Research Briefings – The 1974–1975 UK Renegotiation of EEC Membership and Referendum". Parliament of the United Kingdom. Retrieved 19 May 2016.

"Into Europe". Parliament of the United Kingdom. Retrieved 25 February 2017.

EU treaties". Europa (web portal). Archived from the original on 13 September 2016. Retrieved 15 September 2016.